in the footsteps
of zen

Published by Brolga Publishing Pty Ltd
ABN 46 063 962 443
PO Box 12544
A'Beckett St
Melbourne, VIC, 8006
Australia

email: markzocchi@brolgapublishing.com.au

National Library of Australia
Cataloguing-in-Publication data
     Lim Meng Sing, author.
     ISBN 9780648327776 (paperback)

A catalogue record for this
book is available from the
National Library of Australia

Printed in Australia
Cover design by Brolga Publishing
Typesetting by Elly Cridland
Cover photograph by: Katrina Watson

BE PUBLISHED

Publish through a successful publisher. National Distribution through Woodslane Pty Ltd.
International Distribution to the United Kingdom, North America.
Sales Representation to South East Asia
Email: markzocchi@brolgapublishing.com.au

in the footsteps
of zen

LIM MENG SING, PHD

other books by the author:

The Heart Has Its Reasons:
Poems On Love and Life - A Personal Perspective

Journey Of The Heart
(poems and haiku)

Growing Up In British Malaya:
A Memoir

What Is Love? (An Experimental Project)
(Originator, editor and principal co-author)

Dr. Lim Meng Sing has crafted a beautiful book that honours all that is pure and wonderful in the practice of Zen. *In The Footsteps of Zen* takes the reader on an inner journey of peace and tranquillity, while reminding us that we're inherently connected to our higher Selves and the flow of Life. To remain centred and calm in the midst of a busy (and oftentimes turbulent) world is a challenge for many of us. Dr. Lim has given us a true gem.

Susan Winter,
bestselling author/relationship expert, New York

The author offers a calming voice in the age of anxiety. His book on Zen is, well, very zen and provides a path to deal with the craziness of our times.

John Pomfret,
Pulitzer Prize winner, renowned author of
*The Beautiful Country and the Middle Kingdom:
The US and China, 1776 to the Present*

Dr Lim Meng Sing has written a lucid book on Zen, drawing on his knowledge of its key teachings to provide an inspiring account of the many ways in which it can enrich our spiritual journey and everyday lives. *In the Footsteps of Zen* he succeeds in conveying profound ideas in an approachable and humane fashion. The author draws upon his own life experience as well as upon his extensive reading, to create convincing parallels between Zen and the writing of western authors such as Thoreau and Wordsworth. Dr Lim's own 150 brief, poetic reflections, which make up the second half of the book, provide original, vivid glimpses of the Zen world view. One can imagine readers using them as the basis for their own everyday meditations.

Dr Christopher Ringrose,
lecturer at Monash University, Melbourne,
writer and poet, editor and literary adjudicator
Co-Editor, Journal of Postcolonial Writing;
Co-Editor, Studies in World Literature
(Ibidem Press/Columbia UP),
Creative Lives Project
New book: *New Soundings in Postcolonial Writing*

When everything is nothing
and nothing is everything
that's the moment of truth.

I share the joy and laughter of happy faces,
but sad ones linger for a long time in my mind.

There's a latent candle in every heart
that awaits to be lighted.

Author

In memory of my father
who inspired me to write poetry
and my mother who taught me
patience and humility.

contents

introduction

This is the age of anxiety. This is the age of discontent. This is the age of so much personal dissatisfaction and unhappiness. There is a huge existential vacuum to be filled. Doubt and confusion are everywhere. Joy is missing. Laughter is rare. Life has lost its shine. People are enmeshed in the tedium and humdrum of daily living. Some less fortunate ones are just holding on with no escape route. Despair, disappointment, disillusionment, stress and even depression loom so large in individual lives.

Never has the quest for peace and happiness been so compelling. This is a time for the thinking person to pause, to re-examine his or her values and priorities and to make choices that will restore faith in life and bring meaning.

There is no panacea for our human malaise and there is no quick fix either. But no one need continue to live in misery (economic disadvantages, illness, pain, suffering, tragedy and other adversities aside). The starting point is the individual. And the responsibility and the route to take is not an easy one. However, we should not walk away bereft of hope — we can remake our lives.

Life is all about choices and, if the right choices are made, a better future is attainable.

The most important step that has to be taken is to look at ourselves, as we are, in the present. Are we happy? And if not, why not? What should we do next?

We are all different but are inextricably bound by our common humanity from which we can't escape and which sets the benchmark of our moral behaviour. We are not individual islands but are all citizens of the world and as such have a responsibility to make the world a better place, however small such contribution might be. Through this, we have a larger and wider view of life, other people and the world — we expand, grow and our lives are immensely enriched.

I have written this book as one who has trodden the Zen path for many years, applied its principles in daily living and found fulfilment in this pursuit, but not as a teacher, a role that belongs to the Masters. My 150 reflections on the subject are derived from my personal experiences over a long time.

Following this path has made me a calmer and happier person. I've no doubt what I have been able to achieve others can too, if they would give it a genuine try. To be able to learn, we need, first of all, to be humble.

what is zen?

Mention the word Zen and the listener, in particular the Westerner, immediately connotes Zen with something esoteric, mysterious, steeped in Eastern religion and impenetrable to the ordinary person. Nothing could be further from the truth as Zen is eminently down-to-earth, practicable, secular and relatively 'easy' for a patient, studious, open-minded and unprejudiced person to follow.

There are no dogmas or doctrines in Zen; there is no preaching of religion, no coercion or threat, no compulsion, no prayers to recite, no sanction or judgement, no call to repentance or attributing of blame to anyone, nor any hint of the need for redemption; it is life-and-self-enhancing; it removes doubts and ambiguities; it is humanistic and compassionate; it liberates the false-self. The key word in Zen is 'freedom', achieved through meditation and mindfulness, and practice in everyday life. The most common meditation method is *zazen* (seated meditation).

Being non-religious, non-scriptural and non-doctrinaire, Zen welcomes all people, regardless of their religion or lack of religion, their value-systems, their backgrounds or personal proclivities. Zen and its concomitant 'mindfulness' have swept through the world and captured the heart and imagination of the West since its introduction in the 1950s in the USA, thanks to the pioneering works of D.T. Suzuki and Alan Watts. It was later popularized by Gary Snyder and Jack Kerouac who were associated with the Beat Generation. John Cage found inspiration in Zen which affected the music he composed. Books on the subject have been best-sellers and bear testimony to the ubiquitous acceptance of Zen's humanistic and universal values.

Zen (*Chan* in Chinese 禅) took place in China in the 6th century with the import of Buddhism into the country where it fused with Taoism and blossomed into a school of thought so deep and meaningful that it has awakened the world to a new path, a 'Way' through which peace, harmony, self-integration and happiness can be found by the genuine and persistent practitioner. *Chan* was exported to Korea (called *Son* in that country) and, after that, to Japan from which the word Zen became the standard term that has been used since.

The word 'Zen' means 'meditation' derived from the Sanskrit word *dhyana* (deep concentration).

living in the present

We are the slaves of habit. As John Dryden wrote:
'We first make the habits, then the habits make us.'
We look back to the past, often with regret, remorse, disillusionment or unhappiness — memories, especially painful and hurtful ones, never leave us and return to roost at odd times, especially when we feel unhappy or downcast — we are caught in a vicious cycle and sink into frequent despondency.

Modern life is extremely competitive and stressful. Capitalism is all about material gain and everything boils down to money and profits. Employers ceaselessly and often mercilessly make excessive demands on their staff who must deliver or run the risk of losing their jobs, promotion opportunities or being downgraded. It is fair to say that capitalism, being centered on self-interest and gain, is morally devastating and sometimes demeaning.

No wonder stress, discontent and anxiety abound. Plagued by the past, and faced with an uncertain future, it is very hard for people to concentrate on the present — above all, the extended hours of work and the need to travel long hours to and from work, leave little time for thinking, self-improvement or the family.

We find it very hard to concentrate on the task on hand; we cease to see the wonder and beauty that surrounds us; we worry too much and are easily fatigued; we become irritable and get upset too frequently; our relationships suffer; we have no rest nor do we take holidays; we are stuck to our plight; we feel suffocated; we have lost our sense of direction and *joie-de-vivre*, and are faced by bleakness and futility.

This is where the wisdom of Zen comes into play. We all have choices. We can learn to let go of the past, not to brood about the future and channel our energy and attention to the present.

Carpe diem (seize the day) is from Ode XI of Horace. This saying has been quoted and re-quoted for at least the past 200 years to remind us that the most precious moment open to us is the present. Once it is gone we can never re-live it. We have defaulted on that window of opportunity. Let's quote Horace's statement in full:

> *Dum loquimur, fugerit invida aetas: carpe diem,*
> *quam minimum credula postero*

> *Even as we speak, envious time flies past.*
> *Harvest the day and leave as little as possible for tomorrow.*

The moral here is that the opportunity is now — we should not procrastinate; go for it, do it now lest it be too late; life is short and every moment has to be grasped; *momento mori* (remember we must die); take risks if you must; the doing is the meaning and the liberating.

Zhuangzi (莊子), the most eloquent 14th century BCE follower of Lao-Tzu (老子, 'Wise One') the founder of Taoism, wrote:

> *A path is made by walking on it.*

Forget the years, forget the distinctions. Leap into the boundless and make it your home.

Flow with whatever may happen and let your mind be free. Stay centered by accepting whatever you are doing. This is the ultimate.

mindfulness

Mindfulness through meditation is the heart of Zen. An essential part of meditation revolves around breathing. The practitioner focuses on breathing, the inhale and exhale, the rise and fall of the chest or the sensation in the nose. Constant practice is a *sine qua non* for achieving proficiency and entails the utmost patience.

To be mindful is to focus on and stay with the moment, allowing nothing to distract or come in-between. We put a stop to doing and thinking; we withdraw somewhat; we step back from the world. In the seeming inactivity, a new sensation and experience quietly enter our inner self. Once distraction is out of the way, best achieved through deep meditation, the mind gradually becomes calm and allows the practitioner to have a detached and an unemotional look at himself/herself. The 'What am I?' surfaces; the person looks for his true self, identifies what has gone wrong in his life and the cause of his unrest, discontent or unhappiness that has overwhelmed him for so long and yet won't go away; he will slowly, through mindfulness, come to realize that, as long as he lives only in the external world and neglects his inner world, he will not find the answer to his troubles and will continue to live in misery. He will be surprised and swept along by joy as he progresses in mindfulness as he will come to realize that the more he goes into himself, the more he becomes familiar with his inner self and, in the process, is liberated from his once self-created prison. This is the essence of Zen — the attainment of insight through looking at life and all things with a 'new' mind and through recognizing the wholeness and unity in every phenomenon. It is like a garden that has long been neglected, barren of trees, plants and flowers, over-grown with weeds, coming back into life and abundance and beauty after the absent owner has returned from the faraway and long ago to regain the 'paradise' he once had but, in folly and ignorance, has lost.

Patience, perseverance, dedication and humility — all this is essential for the novice seeking to enter the Zen experience. We are anxious and agitated, busy all the time and have become almost automatons. Deadlines stress us beyond our limits and getting through a single day is a Herculean task.

We have to slow down, to stop or pause, to learn to be quiet and still and to set aside the ineffectual action. The mind that is anchored in the past tends to be muddled and confused. We have to learn to let go of our acculturated mode of thinking; to feel our experience in, and our engagement with, the moment. To create space in which we can expand our consciousness and, in the process, learn how to live, with an empty, unencumbered and 'original' mind is essential.

As we still our mind, clarity sets in and we are surprised to discover that we can 'make a heaven of hell', in the words of John Milton in his epic *Paradise Lost*. In this clarity, we claim back our real, authentic self — life need not be lived in misery anymore. Life and death, sorrow or joy, success or failure, possession or loss, all co-exist and are inseparable; be it good or bad, pleasant or unpleasant, we accept in utmost humility and grace. This is the most important step leading to our liberation and 'enlightenment'.

William Blake's *Auguries of Innocence* is familiar to most of us:

> *To see a world in a grain of sand*
> *And a Heaven in a wild flower*
> *Hold infinity at the palm of your hand*
> *And eternity in an hour.*

And this from Wordsworth's *Tintern Abbey Lines* which is worthy to be quoted at some length for its wisdom and lucidness:

> *These forms of beauty have not been to me,*
> *As is a landscape to a blind man's eye:*
> *But oft, in lonely rooms, and mid the din*
> *Of towns and cities, I have owed to them,*
> *In hours of weariness, sensations sweet,*
> *Felt in the blood, and felt along the heart,*
> *And passing even into my purer mind*
> *With tranquil restoration*
> *Nor less, I trust,*
> *To them I may have owed another gift,*
> *Of aspect more sublime; that blessed mood,*
> *In which the burthen of the mystery,*
> *In which the heavy and the weary weight*
> *Of all this unintelligible world*
> *Is lighten' d — that serene and blessed mood,*
> *In which the affections gently lead us on,*
> *Until, the breath of this corporeal frame,*
> *And even the motion of our human blood*
> *Almost suspended, we are laid asleep*
> *In body, and become a living soul:*

While with an eye made quiet by the power
Of harmony, and the deep power of joy,
We see into the life of things.

Both the romantic poets were describing their experiences soaked in the moment — typically Zen in nature. In the transcendence of such a moment, they saw into the true nature of things without involving their intellect.

The ordinary person might not have heightened moments as intense as the poets' but these experiences are nevertheless open to us all, especially if the person is a lover of solitude and the beauties of nature and willing to set aside time for contemplation.

We should pause a while, then stop and stay in that moment. Listen. Be still. Give up our struggling thoughts. Children are born to live in and love the moment in their unbridled and happy innocence. It is a gift endowed on them by nature. They don't think or reason, they just plunge into the moment, they live it in their fullest here-and-now freedom. They dance, they laugh, they sing, they are not afraid of being what they are. They are immediately spontaneous and pursue what they are doing with undivided attention — they are at one with the environment. That was why Picasso said: ' ... to be creative, we have to be like children (every child is an artist).'

I recently wrote this poem:

Do I need reason
to reason
build for myself
a life-time prison?

Give me the heart
of a child-in every season-
that smile, joy, innocence
no longer would I search for any life-saving beacon.

When we wake up in the morning, our first instinct is to put on the TV or radio or read the papers to start the day — *we have* to know what's happening in the world. Our minds are conditioned this way. Can't we wait? Can't we open the window and admire the first gleam of the sun? Take a short walk in the garden, peep at the trees, plants and flowers and breathe in the crisp morning air, with no distraction? Perchance the buds have bloomed into flowers overnight, new shoots have sprouted, leaves are glittering with dew, a bird may be bursting into song or a gentle breeze may be drifting past. Inspired, we take a walk to a nearby field or park. The morning is beckoning and beauty is just waiting. Then we return home — the aroma of coffee fills the kitchen air and who can resist the tempting smell of eggs and bacon sizzling in the pan? To *be* with the moment is the *real* living!

We have started the day well!

Zhuangzi wrote, so simply but profoundly:

To a mind that is still,
the whole universe surrenders.

And again:

Ten thousand things are insufficient to
distract his (the sage's) mind — that is
the reason he is still.

purpose and meaning

Zen is about the cultivation of fullness of character and the integration of the self without which life would be purposeless and meaningless.

The quest for purpose and meaning is fundamental in the life of the thinking person. Success, power, money or knowledge — all of this doesn't guarantee happiness or fulfilment. But man is weak, selfish, proud, uncaring and seldom thinks of the well-being or welfare of others. The catch-word is: 'Acquire'. And this avarice never stops even if the person in pursuit of such things senses that what he/she is doing or trying to achieve is wrong, immoral or illegal. Very few are not attracted to money and material things. 'If we had more money or material things, we'd be happier' is the common run of thinking. All else is set aside in this pursuit. Philosophical, social and economic research has shown that happiness does not lie in possessions but in contentment, self-fulfilment, duty and service, sharing, love, compassion and reaching out to others and shedding our selfishness and egocentricity — in short, in our very humanity. Such research is based on empirical data and shows that the developed countries, despite their economic growth and prosperity, are still saddled with a host of social and health problems manifested in the high incidence of mental illness, depression, hatred, violence, conflicts and unrests, income and opportunity inequality and crises in human relationships. In the face of progress, our eco-system has suffered immensely and is likely to worsen if this problem is not effectively addressed.

According to the World Health Organisation, depression will be our second most prevalent illness by 2020 — one in five of us will be affected. The social and economic cost will be immeasurable and is the concern of most governments.

Small is more — an expression that's become almost a cliché but is forceful, apt and true. We must learn to be mindful. We are acquiring things that we don't really need but we can't stop ourselves as our philosophy is: 'We must have what our neighbours have; to be left out is to signify we are not successful and people are likely to look down upon us; their kids go to the premiere schools, so ours should too.'

We must keep up with the Joneses, we force ourselves to work harder, longer hours or even take on a second job. We are ready to sacrifice our health and everything else to put ourselves in front of the competition. We fill ourselves with pills, if need be, to keep calm and sane! How right was Thorstein Veblen who invented the term 'conspicuous consumption' in his *Theory of the Leisure Class*: we buy expensive items to display our wealth and income rather than to meet our real needs.

Advertisements are an enemy of our peace of mind. Businesses use the tools of psychology in loud advertisements to brain-wash us: Buy or be unhappy.

This is the message in Vance Packard's *The Hidden Persuaders*. His book was written in 1957 — this trend has accelerated beyond imagination and, with the onslaught of social media, we are all victims somewhat. It's a modern-day malaise that is hard to remove. 'Retail therapy' is a euphemism for 'mass deception'.

Spending on our credit-card is so tempting and no one is immune to it. We pile up debts which grow with time and find it hard to meet repayments — many people apply for more than one card to draw money from the last in order to settle their debts incurred on the first or second card — this is becoming a common scenario. Before long, the problem becomes too huge to be resolved as a vicious cycle has been created. The cause? Greed and discontentment.

We accumulate so many things that our homes become cluttered and too soon we run short of storage space. Then we have to throw some or many things away. What waste! Don't we regret?

The need to de-clutter and downsize is very real and compelling. When you enter someone's home and find that you have difficulty walking into the sitting-room because of the number of things in the way, you can tell immediately it's 'over-stocked'. The owner may be regarded as a 'hoarder' and if you were to enter the store-room, garden-shed or garage, you would see more things being kept there.

This scene comes to my mind: I have visited Japan three times — my first was as a young man of 24. I was fortunate to be invited to the home of a Japanese businessman whose garden consisted of pebbles arranged in circles and nothing else. I didn't know then that it was a Zen garden but I could sense there was calm and peace in that emptiness as there was nothing there apart from pebbles. During my last two trips, the most recent in 2017, I never missed the opportunity of visiting such gardens. Zen is so uplifting and inspiring in its silence, simplicity and such-ness. One could easily miss the beauty of a single flower among a whole field or garden if one were to walk through without a sense of wonder or open awareness. Our minds are just too pre-occupied.

Goodbye, Things (The New Japanese Minimalism) was written by Fumio Sasaki. It turned out to be a best-seller. The author was the former co-editor-in-chief of a Japanese publishing company in Tokyo. He used to compare himself with others and was stressed out. One day, he woke up to the realization that he only had to own things he absolutely needed and in the process got rid of most of the things he owned. Now he lives in a 215 square foot apartment in Tokyo. This has changed his life and opened his mind to the potential of happiness through pursuing a minimalist life. In his book, there are many photos of the room he lives in — every bit of space is put to the maximum use; things are very neatly kept in their respective and seemingly 'right' places; he can locate the items he requires in an instant and saves time and effort; the whole ambience is awesomely Zen. He said goodbye to most of his belongings and emerged a new and contented person.

Sasaki's is a 21st century echo of what Henry David Thoreau, the American transcendentalist, wrote in his classic *Walden* also known as *Life in the Woods*:

Most of the luxuries, and many of the so-called comforts of life, are not only not indispensable, but positive hindrance to the elevation of mankind.

Again:

A man is rich in proportion to the number of things which he can afford to let alone.

Thoreau found meaning in pursuing solitude, simplicity and frugality in the woods of Concord in Massachusetts. He built his own shelter and lived alone earning his livelihood by his own hands. He wrote:

> *I came to the woods because I wanted to live deliberately, to front the essential facts of life, and see if I could not learn what it had to teach, and not, when I came to die, to discover I had not lived.*

> *I never found the companion that was so comfortable as solitude.*

In our blind pursuit of materialism, we have neglected the most important things of life:
love, peace of mind, self-fulfilment, humility, compassion, altruism and our duty to society.

Lao-Tzu wrote:

> *The sage never tried to store things up. The more he does for others, the more he has. The more he gives to others, the greater his abundance.*

simplicity and humility

Zen is emphatic on simplicity and the simple life.
An overgrown garden cannot yield healthy plants and superfluity of material things doesn't make us happier but is also the cause of our unhappiness and discontent.

Lao-tzu wrote:

> *He who knows he has enough is rich.*

But human nature is what it is — adamant and obdurate and strongly antagonistic to change.

The following Chinese proverb puts this succinctly:

> *It's easier to change the course of rivers
> and mountains than human nature.*

The pursuit of and the thirst for pleasure and self-gratification is at the root of human nature and from this entrapment few can escape. 'The simple life' is something that hardly enters our mind and is regarded as alien to our whole concept of living.

Confucius (孔子) wrote:

> *Life is really simple, but we insist on making it complicated.*

Consciously, but almost always unconsciously, we are the product of our environment, its tradition, culture and mores. We are cast in this mould and this is what identifies and defines us. We are enslaved but don't seem to question our existence or what real living means to us. We drift on senselessly and purposelessly.

Henry David Thoreau's most quoted words as contained in his *Walden* still ring so true in our troubled and confused times:

The mass of mankind leads lives of quiet desperation; what is resignation is confirmed desperation.

... I do believe in simplicity. It is astonishing as well as sad, how many trivial affairs even the wisest thinks he must attend to in a day.
... So simplify the problem of life, distinguish the necessary and the real. Probe the earth to see where your main roots run.

This is from Zhuangzi:

Let your mind wander in simplicity, blend your spirit with the vastness, follow along with things the way they are, and make no room for personal views - then the world will be governed.

Fortunately, we all have a choice. Arguably, the simple life is not only meaningful and fulfilling but is also the path to achieving lasting peace and happiness. If we could be content with having enough to eat, a shelter and adequate clothing for the seasons, we would have turned away from the deleterious demands of ambition, fame, success; we would no longer need to compete, to be first in excellence, to be admired or praised, to be the cynosure of society's eyes. Shorn of all that, we would not have frittered our time and energies in blind pursuits; we would cultivate the self; we would devote ourselves to pursuing what is worthwhile, edifying and ennobling; our insight and creativity would have grown; we would live in wonder of and in appreciation of nature's beauty and all the loveliness that exists in the smallest things as what William Wordsworth saw in the 'meanest' flower — the ordinary and humble flower — that 'gave thoughts that do often lie too deep for tears'; we would have time for family and friends and participation in life-enhancing aims and activities of our community; we would like what we do, however humble; we would do our best every day and in fullness of heart and cheerfulness of spirit; we would never shirk our responsibility and duty; we would earn our living from honest and dedicated work; we wouldn't let other people down; we would cultivate sincerity and goodwill; we would practise compassion, kindness and charity; we would be free from envy, prejudice or judging others; in the expansion of ourselves and in our freedom, happiness would not be far away — being and doing, all this makes us truly human — we would have enjoyed a 'well-lived' life.

Living simply and humbly has and will always be the hallmark of excellence and is a trait that belongs to so many great people as exemplified by the lives they lived.

Confucius:

> *The superior man thinks of virtue,*
> *the common man thinks of comfort.*

Albert Einstein:

> I believe that a simple and unsophisticated life
> is the best thing for body and mind.

Henry Wadsworth Longfellow:

> *In character, in manner, in style, in all things,*
> *the supreme excellence is simplicity.*

Isaac Newton:

> *Nature is pleased with simplicity.*

silence

Our daily life is drowned in words and noise — this is the price we pay for our so-called progress. Do we speak because we have something useful to say, or do we speak because we cannot bear to be silent? How many words do we speak a day and how many are superfluous? It's easy to spot a compulsive talker — at work, in the community or at social functions.

Are we content to listen genuinely when others are speaking? Or are we eager to interrupt to have our own say? Many of us, because of our over-active and restless minds, have become automatic talking-machines. It is as though we are pent-up with too many thoughts and need to release them as a safety-valve to effect a catharsis. The word 'listen' contains the same letters as 'silent'! Praise to this tiny but interesting discovery.

One of my friends had a cough that persisted for months and he feared he was suffering from cancer. His throat was tight and his voice was hoarse and he had problems letting the words from his mouth. He consulted a specialist who, after examining him, remarked: 'Your throat and mouth are fine — your problem is that you talk too much and this has strained your larynx!'

The art of purposeful conversation is long-lost and its joy no longer exists when people come together.

Lao-tzu wrote:

> *Those who know do not speak*
> *Those who speak do not know.*

This is from the stoic philosopher Epictetus:

> *We have two ears and one mouth so that we*
> *can listen twice as much as we speak.*

We need silence as never before. It is the key to our health and well-being. Some fifty years ago, I read a medical article, based on research in Germany, that one of the causes of high-blood pressure was noise!

We need space and a quiet environment to find and regain peace. In the cacophony of noise and chatter, we can't find the silence to think, reflect, create and renew ourselves. For the religious, prayer is only possible in silence. Nature's beauty is best appreciated in silence and is marred with any intruding noise. Trappist monks pledge a life to silence and its most vocal member, Thomas Merton, wrote in his *Thoughts in Solitude*:

> *Contradictions have always existed in the soul of [individuals].*
> *But it is only when we prefer analysis to silence that they*
> *become a constant and insoluble problem. We are not meant to*
> *resolve all contradictions but to live with them and rise above*
> *them and see them in the light of exterior and objective values*
> *which make them trivial by comparison.*

Silence has inspired mankind's greatest works. Writers, composers, musicians and artists have withdrawn to a quiet space to do their creative works. Noise would have stifled and suffocated their imagination and creativity.

Meditation is not possible but in silence. Zen believes that understanding, insight and intuition is born from the quiet mind through complete attention being paid to silence and non-attachment. Thus, nothing is as powerful as silence.

I was very fortunate, some fifty years ago, to have discovered Thomas Merton's *Seeds of Contemplation* by sheer chance in a second-hand bookshop. It has been regarded as one of the most influential books of Catholicism. I was completely inspired and enthralled by its humanity and spirituality. Such beauty, lyricism and depth won me over. He brought down barriers between religions and creeds and was in search of forces and threads that bonded all of them together. Sadly, his dream of a spiritual Utopia didn't materialize as he was accidentally electrocuted while staying in a hotel in Bangkok. He had been on a religious tour of Asia talking to religious people. He was only fifty-three.

Merton wrote:

> *In a world of noise, confusion and conflict,*
> *it is necessary that there be places of silence, inner*
> *discipline and peace. In such peace, love will blossom.*

Again:

> *When I am liberated by silence, when I am no*
> *longer involved in the measurement of life, but in the living*
> *of it, I can discover a form of prayer in which there is*
> *effectively no distraction. My whole life becomes a prayer.*

*My whole silence is full of prayer. The world of silence
in which I am immersed contributes to my prayer.*

Merton was a friend of D.T. Suzuki, the great Zen teacher and
was immensely drawn into Zen, despite his training in Catholic
theology and his being a fulltime committed priest living in
Kentucky. His love for Zen inspired him to edit a volume of the
wisdom of Zhuangzi.

Zhuangzi wrote:

*Where is that man who has forgotten words
that I may have a word with him?*

We can feel the immensity of Merton's humility, compassion and
humanity in this statement of his:

*I am able to approach the Buddhas barefoot and undisturbed,
my feet in wet grass, wet sand. Then the silence of the
extraordinary faces. The great smiles. Huge and yet subtle.
Filled with every possibility, questioning nothing, knowing
everything, rejecting nothing, the peace not of emotional
resignation but of Madhyamika (latter schools of Buddhist
philosophy) of sunyata (emptiness or void-ness) that has
seen through every question without trying to discredit
anyone or anything — without refutation — without
establishing some other argument. For the doctrinaire,
the mind that needs well-established positions, such peace,
such silence, can be frightening.*

Nature opens our heart to the reverence of nature, the sanctity of
life, the universe and, verily, to our fellow-men. It's true...

zen as therapy

Z en discovered the subtlety and mystery of the mind long before the advent of neuro-science and its flagstaff, neuroplasticity. I attended two talks given by Dr. Norman Doidge the world-renowned writer on the subject. His book *The Brain That Changes Itself* has been widely acclaimed. He was in Melbourne a few years ago and I met him face-to-face by chance just before the commencement of his first talk. I handed him a short type-written note I had prepared beforehand in which I mentioned something to this extent: that the West, with its orientation on material pursuits, had created its own problems of unhappiness and as such, needed to re-look at itself, concluding that it could benefit from Oriental thinking that was more conducive to peace and happiness. Rudyard Kipling's famous dictum has been proven wrong:

East is East and West is West
And never the twain shall meet ...

There are no barriers to knowledge and wisdom, especially in the present world of digital technology and mass communication — the West has not only found Oriental thinking to be relevant to its way of life but has, in many cases, embraced it with an open heart and mind. This is illustrated by its whole-hearted acceptance and endorsement of Zen as a healing tool, either on its own or as a strong ally or adjunct to Western traditional psychiatric and psychological practices. This has given rise to the emergence of 'Mindfulness-based Stress Reduction' (MBSR) and 'Mindfulness-based Cognitive Therapy' (MBCT) methodologies in the treatment of depression, anxiety, pain, emotional and psychological distress as well as some medical illnesses. The results have been convincing. Both MBSR and MBCT are clinically-based methods of treatment and secular in nature employing manuals and standardized techniques and as such are quantifiable and subject to validity tests. Studies demonstrate both MBSR and MBCT are effective in treating depression and anxiety and help reduce psychological distress. Unipolar depression benefits from MBCT as an adjunctive method of treatment. MBSR helps improve psychological and general health, whether applied to those with psychiatric or psychological conditions or healthy individuals. Zen meditation and MBSR are alternative routes to alleviating pain.

This trend will no doubt gather stronger momentum but will also usher in a period of sustained Eastern and Western dialogue, collaboration and fusion of knowledge for the benefit of all mankind. The impact will be immense as every facet of our human living will be affected. This era of a brave new world is clearly in sight.

Insofar as the general Zen practitioner can find some peace and harmony, he/she will not only be happier, more creative and productive but will also be able to affect others with his/her kindness and compassion.

acceptance of death, grief, suffering and emotional pain

Zen, being derived from Buddhism, teaches impermanence, both of joy and sorrow. Happiness does not last forever, nor does suffering-they co-exist. 'In the midst of life, we are in death', thus speaks *The Book of Common Prayer*, a saying that's known to every Christian. We are human, too human.

Confronted by disappointments, set-backs, and especially pain and suffering, we are thrown off balance. We are lost and hardly know how to speak.

The religious will turn to their faith and no doubt derive some comfort and consolation from this but, for others, they have to struggle on their own, in their humanity, to come to terms with what faces them. Of all the human pains, the loss of loved ones is the most tragic and unbearable.

Suffering — one word — one single experience that shatters the very foundations on which our life rests.

The fear that grips us, the numbness, the emptiness, the dead-end of things, the utter despair and hopelessness — there is no place to escape to, there is no sanctuary or safe place to hide — all that's around us is bleakness complete. Tears, tears and tears-is there any limit to tears in this vacuum of time? Will life ever have any meaning after this?

The rage, the anger, the why?

To be human is to suffer. No one escapes from suffering, whatever form this might take. This is the basic teaching of Buddhism.

How can we cope? How can we have courage and strength? How can we harness our limited human resources to cope with our suffering?

In the immediate present, we stop thinking-our grief takes over and there's nothing that matters beyond this, our darkest hour. Yet, the reality of daily living makes it impossible for us to withdraw totally from life. The daily routine of waking up, eating, taking care of our hygiene, attending to the banalities and chores, being with the family and in touch with relatives and friends, performing our duties and fulfilling our responsibilities loom over us.

Even though this daily living seems painfully difficult at the start we should accept, albeit slowly, what has taken place. To bear our sorrow with dignity, patience and in silence is called for — we should not seek the pity nor sympathy of others, though no doubt some people will hold us close to their hearts. We should abandon self-pity and giving our whole life to mourning or sad memories will only make our life more miserable.

Knowing that suffering and loss is the lot of common humanity gives us a wider and wiser perspective of life and makes our acceptance of suffering easier. Indeed, others have suffered too as we have, perhaps even more and in more tragic circumstances.

By recognizing this, we then find ourselves in the common sea of humanity and, in doing so, find greater strength as we seek to cope with our misery.

Hopefully, we may be somehow transformed. We will no longer think of life in the abstract but wake up to the reality of living. We are mortal and sooner or later we shall die too. This can help us to value life more. If we discard trivia, pettiness and envy and hold to things that are precious and meaningful, this will make us larger than what we are. We will be able to love our dear ones with the fullness of our heart, not just for now but always, without reservation, for we might not have the chance to do so another day. When we do this we acquire humility, the utmost humility. We become quieter and calmer, kinder and more compassionate. We become more responsive to the sufferings of others — even to those whom we don't know or know in passing. Stripped of our egocentricity and selfishness, we are somehow 'born again'. This is growth and it will stay with us for as long as we live. This is the heart and humanism of Zen.

Zen goes further, much further. Life offers no guarantees nor any certainty. Everything is in a flux. Change marks every stage of our life. Everything that is, is itself only a contingency. We are never in control of things. It is this uncertainty that we have to accept as we have no escape route. If we cannot accept uncertainty, our fear and anxiety will always have a hold over us and we will live in fear of losing all that which means the most to us. But what is loss?

We are trapped within ourselves and the more we cling to what we treasure, the more our unhappiness and anxiety grows. Letting go is the hardest thing as we are human and value love and belonging above everything else.

Could we say this: love and beauty are eternal and, once having cultivated these in our heart, they are ours; our very own, to be known or felt by none other except ourselves and as such, can never be taken away from us. It's as though, in our love and adoration of the highest and most sublime sentiments, we somehow rise to a mysterious emotional and 'spiritual' understanding beyond ourselves. If so, we should not rail at destiny nor be bitter — we have had our happy moments, which we knew all along would not be permanent states of existence, and should be humble enough to accept what subsequently follows. To have known love and have dwelt within it is enough blessing for such could have been denied to the less fortunate. We might even say to ourselves: we have been more fortunate than many others.

Wordsworth's poignant *Immortality Ode* speaks of past joy and grandeur lost:

> *Our birth is but a sleep and a forgetting ...*
> *...What though the radiance which was once so bright*
> *Be now forever taken from my sight,*
> *Though nothing can bring back the hour*
> *Of splendour in the grass, of glory of the flower;*
> *We will grieve out, rather find*
> *Strength in what remains behind;*
> *In the primeval sympathy,*
> *Which having been, must ever be;*
> *In the soothing thoughts that spring*
> *Out of human suffering;*
> *In the faith that looks through death*
> *In years that bring the philosophic mind ...*

> *Thanks to the human heart by which we live,*

Thanks to its tenderness, its joys and fears,
To me the meanest flower that blows can give
Thoughts that do often lie too deep for tears.

There is so much of Zen in the heart of Wordsworth. Note the phrase 'the philosophic mind' which might be taken as the mind, which despite loss and suffering, has ascended to a higher spiritual understanding.

In the soothing thoughts that spring
Out of human suffering;
In the faith that looks through death ...

We could say here: acceptance that will give us strength to overcome pain, so we can then move on with courage.

We will grieve not, rather find
Strength in what remains behind ...

Such immortal and humanistic lines!

Viktor Frankl, the founder of logotherapy, wrote in his best-selling *Man's Search For Meaning* that suffering would amount to nothing unless it had a purpose and it was this sense of purpose which marked the humanity and dignity of man. Thus, he postulated that suffering and set-backs were necessary ingredients of a meaningful life. Frankl's logotherapy was life-affirmative and gave hope to those who suffered; man was born to a will-to-meaning, rather than pleasure and this defined him and his worthiness in life.

Life, being transitory, compels us to act responsibly in whatever situation we find ourselves.

Frankl wrote:

> *For the meaning of life differs from man to man, from day*
> *to day and from hour to hour. What matters, therefore, is not*
> *the meaning of life in general but rather the specific meaning*
> *of a person's life at a given moment.*

We should not fear life nor the pain and tragedy that it embodies; we should not fear death either; if we can gain strength to cope with uncertainty and adversity our life will be calmer and kinder. Yes, even as we grieve, we should not despair nor give up living.

Some four decades ago, I stumbled upon Bertrand Russell's *Mysticism And Logic*, which contains a chapter entitled '*A Freeman's Worship*'. In that chapter, he states, in the most beautiful, poetic and poignant language, that man is powerless in the face of fate but can still be larger than tragedy because of his courage as manifested in his resignation to, and acceptance of, what befalls him:

> *To every man comes, sooner or later, the great renunciation ...*
> *By death, by illness, by poverty or by the voice of duty,*
> *we must learn, each one of us, that the world was not made*
> *for us, and that, however beautiful may be the things we crave,*
> *Fate may nevertheless forbid them. It is the part of courage*
> *when misfortunes come, to bear without repining the ruins*
> *of our hopes, to turn away our thoughts from vain regrets.*
> *The degree of submission is not only just and right. It is*
> *the very gate of wisdom ...*

> *From that awful encounter of the soul (in tragedy) with the*
> *outer world, renunciation, wisdom, and charity are born;*
> *and with their birth, a new life begins.*

There is so much of Zen-ness in this piece of Russell's: the acceptance, the renunciation, the humility, the humanity, the fragile state of man as he faces his destiny, his courage in the face of death and pain and suffering.

There is much to learn from Stoicism. Indeed, Russell's article has reflected this. I have benefited profoundly from reading the stoic masters — Marcus Aurelius, Seneca and Epictetus who all taught acceptance of what fate metes out: contentment, a simple life, abandonment of trivia and pettiness, acceptance of uncertainty and the folly of wanting to hold to what we love and desire as a permanent feature of living — for nothing is ever permanent and life, like everything else, is but a contingency. Is this not an echo of Zen?

Even hopes are to be treated with caution. Seneca wrote:

Misfortune weighs most heavily on those
who expect nothing but good fortune.

He wrote further:

It is a great consolation that it is together
with the universe we are swept along.

We have to accept reality with equanimity or be thrown off our equilibrium.

Michel de Montaigne, the 16th century French philosopher was influenced by Stoicism which enabled him to confront death by stripping it of its strangeness and turning it into a commonplace event. He wrote:

It is uncertain where death awaits us; let us await it everywhere.

The French philosopher won't sit still but must be doing something at that hour of arrival:

I want death to find me planting my cabbages, and but careless of death, and still more of my unfinished garden.

What acceptance and serenity! Epicureanism has something to offer as well. According to Epicurus,

... death is nothing to us.

When we exist, death is not; and when death exists, we are not. All sensation and consciousness ends with death and therefore in death there is neither pleasure nor pain. The fear of death arises from the belief that in death, there is awareness.

The Epicureans believed that anxiety had its root in the fear of death and that, if this could be removed, they would be free from fear. They advocated moderation in all things and a balanced, 'agreeable' life based on the 'higher pleasures' such as self-improvement and fraternity.

Zhuangzi's conception of death demonstrates how deep into Taoism he was and how he was able to accept death, not with fear or bitterness, but with the utmost acceptance and tranquillity. Upon his wife's death, he was found pounding upon a tub and singing and, on being asked why he did not weep, he responded:

It's (death's) just like the progression of the four seasons, spring, summer, autumn, winter.

Now she's going to lie down peacefully in a vast room. If I were to follow after her, bawling and sobbing, it would show that I don't understand anything about fate. So I stopped.

How many people would be able to achieve such a high degree of equanimity in the face of death?

Again:

He who has mastered the true nature of life does not labour over what life cannot do. He who has mastered the true nature of fate does not labour over what knowledge cannot change.

Only the rarest of sages could have said this.

Ernest Becker was a renowned cultural anthropologist and the 1974 Pulitzer (non-fiction) award-winning writer of *The Denial of Death* which has been much acclaimed. This was what he postulated:

... man has a symbolic belief system that seeks to transcend his physical and takes on 'immortality projects' (causa sui' projects) to make himself a hero. These works would be seen as part of his immortality and render his life with meaning and purpose in the general scheme of things.

This is an egocentric tendency and a voice that's opposed to that of the Zen spirit although no doubt it appeals to the acquisitive Western mind.

A final note here: Zen teaches us to look beyond our egocentric selves and see life in its true nature. Those who have entered into the *Tao* or Zen bear testimony that this route holds promise of a calmer and happier life. We learn to let go of our self, live in the moment, accept what is meted to us, however painful, without bitterness or rancour, hold our joys lightly as everything in life is transitory, cultivate calmness and peace, embrace simplicity and humility, learn to be content, reach out to others in compassion, to be free from past memories and be fearless of the future. Stripped of our self-absorption and egocentricity, not only are we able to overcome our human vulnerability but we also acquire faith, strength and equanimity of heart and mind. If we can achieve this, we will have assumed a totally new self, and become wholesome in our fullest humanity.

Being humble in our joys, we are more humble when adversity falls upon us. We find peace and our heart opens in compassion for, and sympathy with, our fellow-men.

It is as though we have found 'enlightenment'.

zen and existentialism

Both Zen and existentialism recognize the plight of man in his search for a full understanding of the world and his place in it. To me, the differences are much too wide to be bridged. Existentialism strives to remove the angst, the sorrow, the unhappiness, the emptiness that it regards as innate in life and, as such, freedom and release rest on revolt and action. Albert Camus posed the question: 'What is the meaning of life?' He denied that the question could ever be answered and held that in this vacuum, life's meaning couldn't be found. It was pointless of Sisyphus to bear the weight of the boulder to the top of the mountain only to see it being rolled down as he descended and to be punished by having to repeat that act over and over again for eternity (*The Myth of Sisyphus*). Hence, Camus introduced the idea that existence was 'absurd'. In this absurdity, surely life could not be a 'happy' thing, gloom and despair would be the case. This would be translated into the individual life. While Camus celebrated the universal dignity of man, he was more interested in him as an individual, he saw himself in every man's angst and dilemma. He explained:

If I try to grasp this self of which I am assured, if I try to define it and sum it up, it is no more than a liquid that flows between my fingers ... Between the certainty that I have of my existence and the content that I strive to give to this assurance, the gap will never be filled. Always shall I be a stranger to myself ...

*All the science of this earth will give me nothing that can
assure me that this world is mine ...'*

Camus also wrote:

*... revolt gives life its value ...
(Man must) ... die unreconciled and not of one's own
free will. Suicide is a repudiation. The absurd man can
only drain everything to the bitter end ... The absurd is
his extreme tension, which he maintains constantly
by solitary effort, for he knows that in that
consciousness and in that day-to-day revolt he
gives proof of his only truth, which is defiance.*

Sartre gave voice to his brand of existentialism through his first
novel *La Nausee* (Nauseau) written in 1938 which was regarded
as one of his finest works and a pillar of existential writing. The
protagonist was a dejected French historian who could not define
himself or his own intellectual and psychological freedom. As a
result, he was soaked in nausea which impinged on everything he
did or enjoyed. He suffered from boredom and found no interest in
people despite his effort to find some consolation in their company.
He lacked self-esteem and eventually thought he never existed:

*My existence was beginning to cause me some concern.
Was I a figment of my imagination?*

He sought to revive his relationship with his former lover but was
rejected as she had changed and had moved on with her life.

In psychological terms, the protagonist was suffering from
depression which brought about the nausea. Thus, he personified

the existential condition faced by man in his quest for self, freedom and meaning.

We can see here the plight of the existential seeker as he can't make sense of existence and his life within it — hence the angst and emptiness which must be addressed through revolt and defiance. I regard this as too much self-centredness and man being trapped within his own prison. A key question runs in the veins of existentialists: *What should we do in an absurd world?* The way out is to fight and rebel. The existentialist has to work *against* the emptiness of existence if he is to be able to find happiness and define himself in this inescapable maze of things.

What a despondent and hopeless state of things!

That is the opposite of the pursuit of the Zen-person who doesn't need to fight or rail at existence, nor to deny his rightful place in the universe. He trusts the universe and wants to harmonise himself with it. If he isn't in accord with the universe, he's in ignorance and lives in misery. But he can save himself through finding the right path that's just in front of him; he learns to understand himself through the practice of meditation; he lets go of his past perceptions and replaces them with new ones and, through this, he gains clarity; as he goes deeper into himself, doubt and ambiguity fade away; he is no longer wrapped within himself and has lost his selfishness; he can feel all this in his body and mind and is 'born again'. Through discipline, faith and sincerity, he creates his own salvation. Once he's enlightened, his love and compassion grow and enable him to assume his fullest humanity.

tao te-ching
(道德經 the classic of the way and of virtue)

This classic text constitutes the core ideas of Zen in its fusion with Buddhism.

There are various translations of the title, I shall choose a simple and direct one: *Classic of The Way and of Virtue*. *Tao* means 'the way', *te* means 'virtue', or 'integrity', and *tao-te* as a compound meaning is 'ethics' or 'morality'. *Ching* is 'canon' or 'classic'.

Tao Te-Ching (abbreviated as *Ching* herein) is believed to have been written in 600 BCE. It is one of the most translated books in the world and the most read after the Bible. There have been over 2,400 interpretations of the book of which some 700 are believed to be extant. *Ching* has been translated mainly into English, German and French in the Western world. Despite somewhat differing translations, the basics of the classic have been adhered to and its integrity has been preserved such that Westerners are able to grasp its contents, generally, without much problem. I am fortunate to have had access to a few of these translations over the years.

Ching contains only 5,000 Chinese characters and 81 chapters, also called verses. Its wisdom is conveyed through many paradoxes and challenges the argumentative, disputative and logical mind; *Ching* advocates that we should transcend words, as thinking and articulating words tends to obscure, obstruct, falsify or even tyrannize. It is an invitation to treading another path (way) to achieve clarity, insight and understanding, as every person has an inner self that holds innate and holistic wisdom. In this wholeness, reality and nature are understood, not in fragments, but in fulsomeness and nothing is lacking. The *Tao* is a way of living in consonance with the universe; which translates into the harmony of living with others, the environment and one's own self. In harmony, there is no discord or conflict — life becomes a unity as the oneness of the universe; all that is, is a whole that embraces all parts. In a symphony, every note must fit the whole musical composition and what emerges is a perfect and blissful blend of sounds that transcends the language of words.

It is easy to understand that such a mode of thinking and way of life is alien to and beyond the normal experience of Westerners who are used to the application of reason and logic as they travel through life. The *Tao* then offers an alternative to thinking, feeling, doing and behaving.

Reflections

zen 1
Not to know
but to understand

zen 2
Be the moment
minus yourself

zen 3
Empty
but full

zen 4
The flowers
me in the garden
a bird sings

zen 5
Time knows me
but to it
I don't belong

zen 6

Walking
every step
without thinking
Zen moment in the making

zen 7

Next
but what is next?

zen 8

What is too early?
What is too late?

zen 9

Palms held too tight
no wonder this hurts

zen 10

Zen
no then

zen 11

Is that you?
Is this me?

zen 12

You know?
Who says so?

zen 13

The flowers
in my garden
seem to know me
better than I do myself

zen 14

Wait
wait
wait
and
wait

zen 15

The Zen Master said:
You say you want to be a child
Anyone can say that
Just be one.

zen 16

The sky
knows not its vastness
the sea
knows not its depth

zen 17

The Zen Master said:
You are not ready
to come to me
because your mind is not empty.

zen 18

I
is that me?

zen 19

The Zen Master said:
You've learnt nothing
when you walk from me
every word of mine believing

zen 20

Watering the flowers
just me
and
the flowers

zen 21

Illusion
is always
stronger
than reality

zen 22

You knocked
but no reply
was that the
wrong door?

zen 23

Listen
not just for now
listen wherever you are
in every season

zen 24

Deem yourself
fortunate
as no one
spoke to you today

zen 25

Thousands of trees
rustling in the forest
all at the same time
can you tell which?

zen 26

Enlightenment
has no time-table
mysteriously it dawns on its own
– you can't enable

zen 27

Know that
truth resides
not in the visible shell
but in the hidden kernel

zen 28

The Zen Master said:
Speak clearly
use simple words
avoid long sentences.

zen 29

A rose
can't be more
or less than a rose
accept it as it is
or walk away

zen 30

The Zen mind
abhors reason
it does not seek
to define

zen 31

The Zen Master is asleep
do not wake him
his eyes are closed
but he can see

zen 32

The Zen Master said:
First lesson: be patient.

zen 33

The Zen Master said:
Do not think the smartest I prefer
all I ask for is a humble and sincere heart
such is less likely to err.

zen 34

Insight can't be found
from what's in sight
it resides –
in your hidden inside

zen 35

The Zen Master said:
Do not come thinking,
when you leave here
you should give up reasoning.

zen 36

Do not ask for more
but rather for
the little
that's enough

zen 37

Reading a poem
in my garden yesterday
myself I forgot
something took me faraway

zen 38

Don't pay attention
to the 'I'
a new self you will discover
as each moment passes by

zen 39

Because it is
it can't be is-not

zen 40

The happiest traveller
travels with the least luggage

zen 41

Imagine
you are a tiny leaf
floating effortlessly
in a calm stream

zen 42

You have no business
to look across your neighbour's fence.

zen 43

The Zen Master said in class:
Your will is not enough
it has to be coupled with
patience and humility.

zen 44

The Zen Master said:
This morning I walked in the garden
I saw dew shimmering on the leaves
tell me tomorrow what you see.

zen 45

The Zen Master said:
I don't ask you
not to suffer when you must
all that I can say is this:
Zen can help you understand
the meaning of suffering and pain.

zen 46

Zen is timeless
for the follower
who lives in every moment

zen 47

The Zen Master said:
Your mind you over-load
in its congestion
it slips into imbalanced mode.

zen 48

There's plenitude
in emptiness

zen 49

Late at night
you knocked at my door
'Come, share my supper
though I am poor.'

zen 50

Zen is not about
accumulating
but about
emptying

the mind
is like a room
once too cluttered
chaos it does assume

zen 51

Zen shows the way
to harmonious living
and prepares one for accepting dying

zen 52

A time to celebrate
a time to weep
a time to embrace
then enter into non-returning sleep –

be with the moment
the mystery deep
while the mind questions
in vain – faith and enlightenment leap

zen 53

Minus 'I'
add humility
multiply its plenitude
then divide
among common humanity
for the heart of Zen
is compassion, kindness
selflessness, humility
we are all bound together
as a universal family –
Zen the gateway
to peace and harmony

zen 54

Simplicity is too hard
for many people
as they take delight
in things that impress others

zen 55

Am I not fortunate
in having little
as there's enough food
on my table while others have none?

zen 56

Zen has neither doctrines nor dogmas
as such, it's eminently practical and practicable
there's no place designed for worship
the moment and acceptance is living total

zen 57

Reason sees only partially
Zen removes ambiguity

zen 58

Fear arises from insecurity
if one is empty
and owns and holds to nothing
one fears no loss
in any eventuality

zen 59

Keep in your heart
just a few words
turn to them
in your suffering and sorrow
live by just
those few words

zen 60

A student asked the Zen Master:
Master, how do I live simply?

Answer:
Don't burden yourself
with wanting and owning – be desire-free.

zen 61

Come
O calm
be my peace
be my outcome

zen 62

The sharper eyes
are within the heart
the outer sight eludes
from truth it's far apart

zen 63

Silence
the respite
from words –
an awakening

zen 64

Nothing
is promised
nothing
is demanded

every Zen student
charts his own path
in the world
that's unbounded and unencumbered

zen 65

Doubt arises
from reasoning
Zen circumvents logic
triumphs through intuiting

zen 66

When the mind is empty
the dross drops away
beyond ambiguity
the Zen adherent doesn't go astray

zen 67

Holding a fishing rod
with no string nor bait
over the stream hoping
to see a fish appearing

zen 68

A moonless and starless night
in the dark I walked
not knowing why I was out
for so many long hours

zen 69

In aloneness
in stillness
watching the flowing sea
I forgot my hunger

zen 70

Expecting nothing
the moment unthinking
words vanishing
silence all-embracing

zen 71

The first Zen lesson
The Master said:
Before you sit down
remove everything from your pocket!

zen 72

The lightest breeze
can cause a ripple
the slightest word
can stir up trouble

zen 73

Zen
has a beginning
but knows
no ending

zen 74

Listening not with the ear
but with the heart
the eye sees 'something'
Zen sees the whole 'thing'

zen 75

The mind
crystal-clear
asks no questions
lives in the now and here

zen 76

Yesterday's joy
I tried to recapture today
but couldn't
it had overnight slipped away

zen 77

In Zen
there's nothing
to repent
emptiness all-pervading

zen 78

So said the Master of Zen:
I'd prefer that you walk than run
in your haste you miss the trees
for the forest and have lost the fun.

zen 79

When
would you
enter
the moment Zen?

zen 80

The student rushed
to the Zen Master and exclaimed:
I'm enlightened!

The latter remarked with an avuncular smile:
Sixty years I've laboured
that sentence I still can't utter!

zen 81

The mind reasons
but the heart understands

zen 82

Zen has no address
nor dwelling-place
you can get in touch
at any time or place

zen 83

Zen
is
the means
also the end

zen 84

Zen
the instant
all else
is distant

zen 85

If you've got rid
of the fear of losing
that's the beginning
of your self-awakening

zen 86

In the sun
the wood-cutter
chopped wood
the rain came
he hid under a tree
when it stopped
he started all over
again
not for a moment
did he complain

zen 87
The Zen master said to the students:
Go to the beach tomorrow
pick up the first shell you come across
look beyond no more

zen 88
The blacksmith
the work-shop
the sound of cutting machines
they become the moment

zen 89
Zen
just think of it
as an
open window

zen 90
Zen
silence
in wordlessness
there's no sentence

zen 91
Should everything
have a reason?

zen 92
The true Zen-person
should be larger than death
he does not have to reason
he has mastered all in each breath

zen 93
Unfazed
unmoved
empty of thought
doubts removed

zen 94
People are unhappy
they pursue the illusory
they forget the intrinsic
and authentic

zen 95
Your mind is full
but your heart is starved
you have lost life's essence
rocks are not meant to be carved

zen 96

The Zen Master said:
Mine are words –
the hard work is yours –
yours alone –
do not forget

zen 97

You are
your own master
and salvation
none other

zen 98

I lost
because
I was out
looking
for the wrong thing
when the right thing
was
just
before my eyes

zen 99

The student said to the Zen Master:
Master, five years I've been here
so little I've learnt
can I make it? I do fear.

The Master replied:
The seed becomes the root
the root becomes the shoot
the shoot becomes the tree.
Don't you know
you started life
as a baby?

zen 100

Happiness you guard so jealously
as though it's a bird that would fly away
hold it lightly and in humility
you can't force it to stay

zen 101

What you are
is not tested in your prosperity
but in your destitution, loss
and times of adversity

zen 102

Having entered
Zen's emptiness
I am full –
beyond
sadness and happiness

zen 103

The Zen Master said to the students:
If you are here to judge or impress
you are at the wrong place
all that I teach is egoless-ness

zen 104

Z for Zero
E for Emptiness
N for nothingness

zen 105

Letting go
my false hero
that stubborn
Ego

zen 106

Zen leads you
to your inner core
if you know yourself
you need little more

zen 107

Zen
is simply
the way
to see clearly

zen 108

Letting go –
life's hardest lesson
people are habits – ingrained
they create their own prison

zen 109

How sublime
it is to recognize
that there's
no such dimension as time

zen 110

Zen
is
when
I lose myself

zen 111

The Zen mind
is an empty chamber
free and unencumbered
is its owner

zen 112

Thinking suspended
muddling no longer vexes –
in the sea of tranquillity
the mind is free from any nexus

zen 113

The Zen Master said to the students:
Don't compare with your fellow-students
Zen is all about your journey alone
think not about progress or enlightenment
the prize is living in the moment

zen 114

The green field
beneath the still clouds
the murmur of the wind
nature knows no doubts

zen 115

Before I walked the Zen Way
troubles followed me everywhere
now, nestled in its cradle
my mind is clear anywhere

zen 116

The Zen Master said to the students:
Nothing is permanent
everything is transient
holding on to nothing
the moment reveals its true meaning.

zen 117

Me
the morning
the inter-facing
is the day's meaning

zen 118

It's not what you see
but how
enlightenment
is seeing clearly in the now

zen 119

In the emptiness of Zen
there's nothing for me to choose
preference or selection doesn't arise
neither is there anything to refuse

zen 120

Zen-the inner eye
that ignores the 'I'

zen 121

One word
spoken or written
invites more words
beginning of confusion

zen 122

What's the shape
and colour of illumination?

zen 123

How do you measure emptiness?

zen 124

Beware of eagerness
it's a sign of impatience
be of calmer nature
you would be rewarded by patience

zen 125

Zen is
less about doing
and
more about undoing

zen 126

That silence
I need
nothing more
that's what will bring me
from the tumultuous sea
to the tranquil shore

zen 127

What is
the core of Zen?
It is that unity
within you –
being un-fragmented
devoid of definition
analysis or question
you dwell in blissful harmony
in silence and wordlessness
anchored in the immediacy
of the very moment
without the interference
of the future
nor memory
of the gone-before

zen 128

This is the problem
with the mind
it tortures itself
with thoughts
of the future
and events
it had left behind

zen 129

The Zen Master said to the students:
It means nothing to me – your intelligence
all that I wish of you all is
humility, attention and patience.

zen 130

Zen
is not a mood
but a state of being
it cuts away time
and memory
clear and calm
becomes its seeing

zen 131

Upon awakening in the morning
I prepared my cup of coffee
the aroma filled the kitchen
I forgot it was a working-day

zen 132

Zen
discriminates not
without judging
it bears no hurtful thought

zen 133

The restless mind
has lost its way
the owner leaves it behind
and walks into the new day

zen 134

Where's the home
of the Zen mind?
it's the universe entire
its past home it has left behind

zen 135

Because you are not still
and can't let go
you turn your head
the immediacy is gone — lo!

zen 136

Why me?
The world
could manage
so easily
on its own
minus me

zen 137

I have no business
beyond what
I am doing now

zen 138

The same old fisherman
pushes his boat to the sea
never does he even once fail
to look at the morning sky

zen 139

The dew falls
on the leaf
of the tree
in the garden

the Zen Master
stops. He looks
in wonder
he is at one
with the dew
the leaf
the tree
but forgets
he's in the garden

zen 140

Next
what next?
it's the present
still
the present –
don't anticipate

zen 141

Little is
over much
Zen is
such

zen 142

In the emptiness of things
inscribe your story
it's you and that nothingness –
nothing more beyond – that inter-facing only

zen 143

The real me
what could that be?

zen 144

Ancient Greek maxim:
Know thyself'
Zen's central dictum:
Untie yourself'

zen 145

Doing away with the dualistic mind
Zen accepts life's transience happily
death is deemed as part of living
this it is ready to embrace with tranquillity

zen 146

By the window, sitting
it's raining
I listen to the sound
doing nothing

zen 147

This is the problem
with words – the essence
of things eludes them
true meaning is in absence

zen 148

Too many people
live in regret
unable to let go
they can't forget

zen 149

Zen dispels
distraction
it is sharply-focused
attention

zen 150

The barriers of my mind
have been brought down
I have a clarity I can't define
experiencing and living in the now

about the author

The author has been exposed to Zen for some four decades, as well as to the teachings of Buddhism, Taoism and Confucianism. At the same time, he has been profoundly affected by Western thinking.

In his memoir, he wrote:

*'The Western mind is liberal and the Chinese and Eastern,
contemplative, and both cultures invite me into their
infinitely rich and splendid worlds.
From either garden, I can pick up the most beautiful flowers
and the fountain of wisdom is never dry — therein I drink
the purest water to my heart's content'.*

Lim Meng Sing grew up in what was then called Malaya, which was under British rule at that time. A precocious child, he was instinctively drawn to English poetry and began writing poems for the school magazine when he was twelve. 'It was the start of my journey into the greatest joy of my life, which coincided with my passion and love of Western classical music and Latin.'

Lim received his Ph.D (*avec la mention bien*) from the Catholic University of Paris in 1974. He is the founder of The Melbourne Circle modelled after The Bloomsbury Group of 20th century London.

Apart from being a writer, Lim is a self-taught composer and violinist and, in his spare time, performs for charities.

The author lives with his wife of 54 years in Melbourne. They have two grown-up sons and two grandchildren.

in the footsteps of zen
Lim Meng Sing

			Qty
ISBN: 9780648327776			
	RRP	AU$19.99	.....
Postage within Australia		AU$5.00	.....
		TOTAL* $_____	
		* All prices include GST	

Name:..

Address: ....

....

Phone: ....

Email: ....

Payment: [ ] Money Order   [ ] Cheque   [ ] MasterCard   [ ]Visa

Cardholder's Name:..

Credit Card Number: ....

Signature:..

Expiry Date: ....

Allow 7 days for delivery.

Payment to: Marzocco Consultancy (ABN 14 067 257 390)
                            PO Box 12544
                            A'Beckett Street, Melbourne, 8006
                            Victoria, Australia
                            admin@brolgapublishing.com.au

Be Published

Publish through a successful publisher.
Brolga Publishing is represented through:
• National book trade distribution, including sales,
marketing & distribution through Woodslane Pty Ltd
• International book trade distribution to:
  - The United Kingdom
  - North America
  - Sales representation in South East Asia
• Worldwide e-Book distribution

For details and enquiries, contact:
Brolga Publishing Pty Ltd
PO Box 12544
A'Beckett St
Melbourne, Vic 8006
markzocchi@brolgapublishing.com.au
(Email for a catalogue request)